Light Your Way:
Make a Candle

By Carla Mooney

Norwood House Press
PO Box 316598
Chicago, Illinois 60631

For information regarding Norwood House Press, please visit our Web site at:

www.norwoodhousepress.com or call 866-565-2900.

Picture Credits:
cc-by-sa3.0*/Akiyoshi's Room/Wikimedia, 21; Asif Akbar, 14 (left); István Benedek, 25; cc-by-sa3.0/Andrea Schaufler/Wikimedia, 14 (right); Nerry Burg, 16; Christian Carollo, 22 left; Wendy Dinkel, 5; © Alain d'ORTOLI, 42; Anthony Eden, 11; Fran Gambín, 7; Nikita Golovanov, 10; Bonnie J, 23; Milda K, 6; Aron Kremer, 13 left; cc-by-sa2.0/Paul Maingot/Wikimedia, 20; © Geoffrey Métais, 24; Carla Mooney, cover, 30-32, 38, 40 (right); © Mozzyb/Dreamstime.com, 26; cc-by-sa3.0/Henry Mühlpfordt/Wikimedia, 18; Christopher Myers/USAF photo, 13 (right); National Oceanic & Atmospheric Administration (NOAA), 9 (left), 10; Joseph Paris, 28, 29, 34, 36, 37, 39, 40 (left), 41; Public Domain/Wikimedia, cover (background), 8, 9 (right); Dariusz Rompa, 22 (right); cc-by-sa3.0/Secretlondon/Wikimedia, 12; Laura Shreck, 15; cc-by-sa3.0/Stilfehler/Wikimedia, 17; Gnu Free Documentation/Zenodot Verlagsgesellschaft mbH/Wikimedia, 4
*cc-by-sa= Creative Commons by Share Alike License

LIBRARY OF CONGRESS CATALOGING-IN-PUBLICATION DATA

Mooney, Carla, 1970-
  Light your way : make a candle / Carla Mooney.
    p. cm. -- (Adventure guides)
Includes bibliographical references and index.
  Summary: "Explores the history and science of candle making. Includes step-by-step instructions for making beeswax and milk carton candles. Other topics include decorating candles and safety. Glossary, additional resources and index"--Provided by publisher.
  ISBN-13: 978-1-59953-387-2 (library edition : alk. paper)
  ISBN-10: 1-59953-387-1 (library edition : alk. paper)
1. Candlemaking--Juvenile literature. I. Title.
  TT896.5.M68 2010
  745.593'32--dc22
                                                        2010010399

Manufactured in the United States of America in North Mankato, Minnesota.
158N—072010

Table of Contents

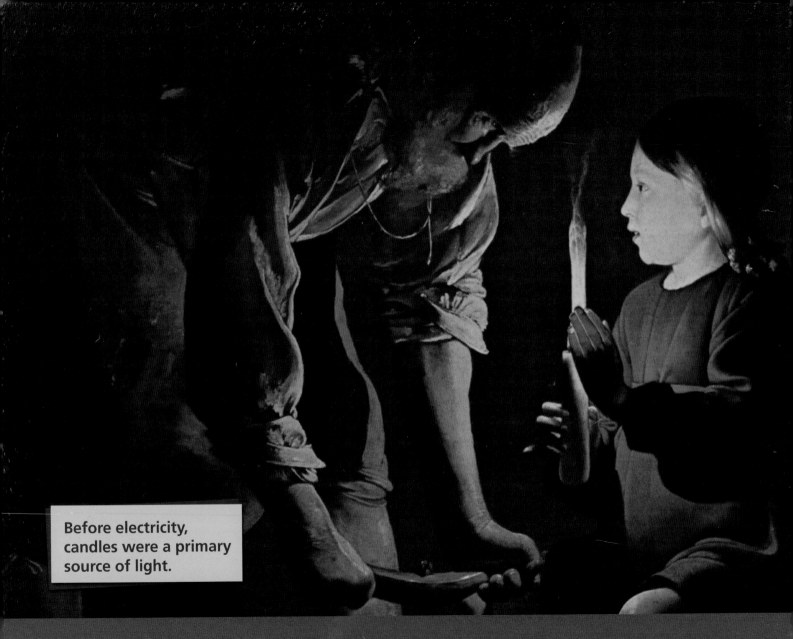

Before electricity, candles were a primary source of light.

Candles:
Lighting the Dark

If the electric lights suddenly went out in your home, you would probably light some candles until the electricity came back on. Like many people in the past, the candle would be your main source of light after the sun set.

The word *candle* comes from the Latin word *candere*. It means "to shine or be bright." A candle is a solid chunk of **tallow** or wax wrapped around a **wick**. Wax is a solid substance that is similar to fat, but it is less greasy and more **brittle**. Wax also melts easily when heated. Some waxes are found naturally in plants and animals. Other waxes, such as paraffin, are human-made. When the candle's wick is lit with fire, the candle shines as a source of light.

Candles are fun and easy to make.

Early Candles

People have always needed a source of light. Although the history of candle making has not been recorded, it is believed that the ancient Romans were the first to develop a candle with a wick. For their wicks, they chose natural fibers like **flax**, hemp, or cotton.

Flax was used to make candlewicks.

Then they melted tallow and poured it over the wick to form the candle. These early tallow candles had many uses. The Romans burned candles to light their homes and to help with nighttime travel. They also burned candles in ceremonies. Despite their usefulness, tallow candles had drawbacks. They often burned poorly and gave off a **rancid** odor.

Other people made early candles from plants. Dried vegetable fibers, sticks, or flax threads became wicks. People dipped these natural materials into **pitch**, fat, resin, tar, or wax to create a candle. In China candle makers molded rice paper into tubes to make a wick. Then they created a wax from an insect and seed mixture. In India people boiled the cinnamon tree's fruit to make candle wax.

The Middle Ages

During the Middle Ages Europeans discovered that beeswax made better candles than tallow. Beeswax is a substance **secreted** by honeybees to make their honeycombs. Unlike tallow, a beeswax candle does not smoke. It also has a pleasant smell. Yet beeswax was not as plentiful as tallow. That made beeswax more expensive. Only wealthy people and churches could afford beeswax candles. Therefore, most Europeans continued to burn tallow candles.

Using beeswax to make candles is easy, but the substance is not as plentiful as human-made materials.

By the 13th century, candles were **indispensable** in most European homes. Candle makers were called chandlers. To make candles, they dipped wicks into melted tallow or beeswax. They also poured wax repeatedly over wicks

Timekeepers

In ancient times people used candles to measure the passing of time. Because a candle burned consistently, they knew how far it would burn in one hour. To measure time with a candle, they marked hour-long intervals in the candle wax.

The candle was also a primitive alarm clock. First, the user put a nail in the candle wax and placed the candle in a tin pan. When the wax melted down to the nail, the nail would clatter into the pan, sounding its alarm.

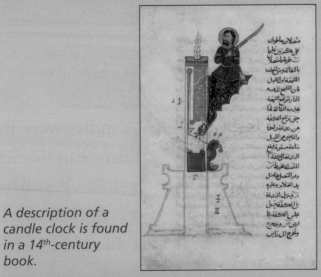

A description of a candle clock is found in a 14th-century book.

until a thick coating of wax built up. By the 15th century, chandlers developed wooden molds to form tallow candles. This made tallow candles easier to make and more affordable. Nonetheless, it did not change their drawbacks. They still burned quickly, and their wicks had to be trimmed frequently to prevent smoking.

Colonial Times

During the 18th century, whalers crystallized sperm whale oil to create spermaceti wax. They chilled the crude sperm oil until the spermaceti wax separated and **congealed** into a white, waxy solid. This wax had several advantages for candle making. Like beeswax, it did not smell when burned. It also produced a significantly brighter light than beeswax or tallow candles. The spermaceti wax was harder than tallow and beeswax. It did not soften or bend in summer heat. In addition, it was easy to make in large quantities. This made spermaceti wax candles very affordable.

Workers process whale spermaceti to remove the oil. Before electricity, whales were hunted to obtain their oil.

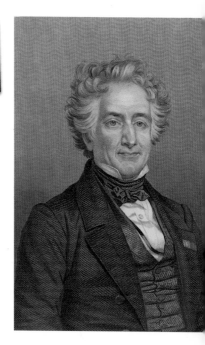

French chemist Michel Eugene Chevreul

19th-Century Advances

During the 19th century, several advances in wax and candle making further improved candles. In the 1820s French chemist Michel Eugene Chevreul discovered how to extract **stearic acid** from animal fat. This led to the development of stearin wax. Candles made from stearin wax were harder and burned longer and cleaner than unrefined tallow candles.

Candlefish

The candlefish is a type of smelt fish, which is a small, silvery fish found in the ocean off the Pacific Northwest coast of the United States. The candlefish is full of fat and oil. When dried and strung on a wick, it can be burned from end to end like a candle. Native Americans in the Pacific Northwest used candlefish by putting a stick into the oily dried fish and lighting it.

A candlefish made for an easy source of light for Native Americans.

In the 1850s chemists separated a waxy substance from petroleum and refined it into paraffin wax. Paraffin burned cleanly and had no odor. It was also the cheapest candle wax to make.

One disadvantage of paraffin was that it was very soft so it had a low melting point. To solve this problem, candle makers added stearic acid to the paraffin wax. The acid hardened the soft paraffin. Many of today's modern candles are still made with a combination of paraffin and stearic acid.

Also during the 19th century, Joseph Morgan invented a machine that could continuously make candles. Morgan's machine was a cylinder with a movable **piston**. The piston ejected candles from the cylinder as they solidified. Before Morgan's machine, candle makers slowly formed candles by hand. Now a machine could make candles faster and more efficiently. This meant that candles would become more affordable for the average person.

In 1879 Thomas Edison introduced the electric lightbulb to the world. His invention dramatically affected the use of candles. Electric lights quickly replaced candles as the most popular source of light. As a result, candle making declined.

More Than a Source of Light

Although candles are no longer a major source of light, they remain an important part of traditions, cultures, and religions around the world. Lighting a candle often has **symbolic** meaning. On a birthday cake, candles represent how old you are. At some weddings, a

Candles are used in many celebrations.

unity candle lit by the bride and groom symbolizes their joining as a married couple. Lighting a candle is also a simple way to remember loved ones who have died. During protests or awareness events, hundreds of people light candles to symbolize unity. Many candles lit at the same time and place attract attention to their cause.

Candles in Religion

Candles play an important role in religious ceremonies around the world. Candles are a traditional part of many Buddhist rituals. The candle's light represents the light of Buddha's teaching. As a show of respect, a candle often is placed with incense and flowers in front of a Buddhist **shrine** and images of Buddha.

In the Hindu religion, a diya, or clay lamp, is an important part of religious and social rituals and rites. It symbolizes enlightenment and prosperity. Traditionally, a diya is made from baked clay. It holds oil or wax that is lit with a cotton wick.

Candles also are a central part of many Jewish holidays and festivals. One of the most well-known Jewish holidays is Hanukkah, or the Festival of Lights. During Hanukkah a special candleholder called a menorah holds eight

(Right) During Kwanzaa, one candle is lit each night in a holder called a kinara.

(Below) One candle is lit in a menorah each night during Hanukkah.

candles and a special candle called the *Shamash*. For eight nights, Jews use the Shamash to light a new candle in the menorah.

Kwanzaa celebrations also use candles. Kwanzaa is an African American holiday that runs from December 26 to January 1. During Kwanzaa a candle-holder called a kinara holds seven candles. There are three red candles, three green candles, and one black candle.

Types of Candles

Do you know the names of different types of candles?

- Container candles are poured into a special glass or piece of pottery.
- A votive candle is a small, cylinder-shaped candle that is placed in a small cup or votive holder. Votives were originally made white and unscented for use in religious ceremonies. Now they are available in all different colors and scents.
- A pillar candle is freestanding and at least 3 inches (7.6cm) in **diameter**. It can be round, square, or hexagonal in shape.
- A taper ranges from 6 inches to 20 inches (15.2 to 50.8cm) tall. It is sometimes called a dinner candle.
- A small, cylindrical tea light candle is poured into a metal holder. The tea light is about 1.5 inches (3.8cm) high and 1 inch (2.5cm) in diameter.

A pillar candle

Each candle represents one of the seven principles, or values, of Kwanzaa. During the celebration a different candle is lit each night.

In Christian religions candles represent the light of God or the light of Christ. Candles often are carried in processions and are placed in pairs on altars. During ceremonies such as bap-

These candles are arranged to celebrate Advent. A white Christ candle can be added in the middle at Christmas.

tisms, funerals, and first communions, candles also are lit. Christmas celebrations frequently use candles. In Western churches four candles arranged in a wreath represent the weeks in the **Advent** season. In Western Europe some Christians burn an Advent candle in their homes to count down the days until Christmas. Before electric lights were invented, people also used candles to light and decorate Christmas trees.

The Eternal Flame

People have burned candles for thousands of years. Although in most places they are no longer an important source of light, candles are still incredibly popular. Candles decorate homes with a warm glow. People of all faiths and backgrounds burn candles as they worship, celebrate, and grieve. For many, the candle's flame sends a message of hope, faith, warmth, and security.

The lighting of candles can be the center of many personal rituals.

In chapter 4, you will learn to make candles shaped with a milk carton.

Chapter 2

Flickering Flames:
How Does a Candle Work?

Wax is the candle's fuel. At room temperature wax is solid. Yet when heated, it melts to a liquid. Today paraffin is the most common candle wax used around the world. In smaller amounts, beeswax also is used for candles. Stearin wax is used mostly in European candle making. Other candle waxes include soy, palm, and **synthetic** waxes.

The wick is the candle's most important part. A wick is a bundle of fibers that are twisted, braided, or knotted to-gether. These fibers absorb the liquid wax and carry it to the flame. There are more than one hundred types of wicks. Each has a different size, shape, and material. Picking the right wick for a candle helps it burn cleanly and at the right pace. If the wick delivers the candle fuel to the flame too quickly, the candle will

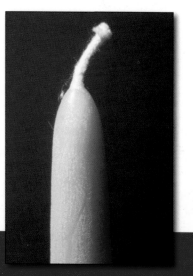

This homemade candle uses a cotton wick.

Burn Rate

Different wicks and waxes affect how fast a candle burns. Most people prefer to buy long-lasting candles. As a result, candle makers want to make candles that burn slowly. To measure how fast a candle burns, they calculate the candle's burn rate.

To calculate the burn rate, first weigh the candle. Next, burn the candle for a set length of time. Then snuff the candle and reweigh it with any drippings. Dripped wax is considered unburned. This is because the candle's flame did not use it as fuel. By comparing the starting and ending weights, you know how much of the candle was burned. You can then figure out how much was burned per minute. Consider this example: A candle weighs 500 grams. After burning for one hour, the candle weighs 140 grams. Therefore, the candle burned 360 grams (500 minus 140) in sixty minutes. The candle's burn rate is 6 grams per minute (360 divided by 60).

To make your candle, you will need to choose a material to make a wick.

flare and produce **soot**. If the wick delivers the fuel too slowly, the candle's flame will flicker out.

How a wick is made affects how it burns. Braided wicks burn slowly and steadily. Most of today's wicks are braided or knotted fibers. Twisted wicks burn much faster. Their loose construction carries more fuel to the flame quickly. Fast-burning twisted wicks are commonly used in birthday candles. Some wicks are also soaked in a fire-**retardant** solution. This causes the wick to burn more slowly, making the candle last longer and burn more evenly.

In addition to wax and wicks, candle makers use dyes and pigments to create candles in a rainbow of colors. Pigments are coloring particles that do not dissolve in water, oil, or other liquids. The pigment particles lie in a film on the sur-face of the object they color. In general, pigments do not burn well. This makes them best suited to coat the outside of a candle with color. Unlike pigments though, dyes dissolve in liquids. Dyes burn easily and can be used to color a candle throughout its entire body, not just its surface.

Pigments sit in bins in a store.

Many types of candles are displayed in this candle factory and store.

How a Candle Is Made

Most candles are made by placing a wick into wax. Then the candle maker forms the wax in different ways to create the candle's shape and size.

- *Cast and molded.* The candle maker pours wax into a mold or shape and places a wick in the wax. Molds can be metal, plastic, or rubber. They also can be made from common items like empty milk containers.

- *Dipped.* The candle maker repeatedly dips a wick into a container of melted wax. Over time the wax builds in layers on the wick. Dipping creates a natural taper-shaped candle.

Fragrance is a common ingredient added to wax to make candles smell good. When the fragrance evaporates from the hot liquid wax, the candle's scent is released into the air. Most candle fragrances are made from essential oils or synthetic chemicals.

- *Drawn*. The candle maker pulls long pieces of wick through melted wax. This works well for small, thin candles like birthday candles.
- *Poured*. These candles are made by pouring wax repeatedly over a wick until a candle is built up to the desired size.

A candle-making workshop in Japan shows the tools of the trade.

- *Rolled*. These candles are made by rolling sheets of wax around a wick. This method creates tapers and pillar candles.

A Chemical Reaction

A candle burns when the heat of the flame melts a small pool of wax around the wick. The wick's fibers soak up the liquid wax and carry it to the flame. The wax fuels the flame and keeps it burning.

Melted wax surrounds the wick of this candle as it burns.

is exothermic. That means it releases heat into the air.

The amount of oxygen in the air affects how fast a candle burns. Without enough oxygen, the flame will sputter out. More oxygen causes the flame to burn brighter and more quickly. Oxygen levels are generally greatest on the outer edge of a candle's flame. This makes the flame's edge the hottest part of the candle.

Near the wick, the melted wax breaks down and releases hydrogen

The candle wax is a **hydrocarbon.** When candle fuel burns, it reacts with oxygen and releases carbon dioxide and water vapor into the air. These are the same by-products that humans exhale when breathing. This chemical reaction

Candle flames are affected by wind.

Why Do Candles Drip?

Have you ever had a candle that dripped hot wax? You are not the only one; most people have this candle experience. Here are some tips to figure out why your candle is dripping and how to avoid it:

1. Drafts can cause candles to drip. Make sure you burn your candles away from drafty places, such as near an open window or a fan.
2. Make sure you have enough time to burn your candle. The minimum amount of time a candle should burn is one hour per inch (2.5cm) of diameter. The candle needs to burn long enough so that the melted wax spreads to almost the full diameter of the candle. This is especially important on the candle's first burn.
3. Do not burn your candle too long. This may cause the candle walls to become misshapen. If the pool of wax grows too big, it can melt a hole through the wall of the candle. This will cause wax to drip down the candle's side. You should extinguish the flame as soon as the wax pool approaches the candle's outer edge.

Burning too long causes this candle to drip and become misshapen.

Smoke from these candles is caused by unburned soot.

and long carbon chains that produce light. The carbon chains get so big that they become tiny particles of soot. The soot particles burn and produce the candle flame's yellow light. If the candle is burning properly, the soot particles burn up in the flame. If the candle burns quickly, from too much oxygen or wax, some unburned soot particles escape the flame. When this happens, the candle smokes. Smoking can also happen if the wick is too long or if a breeze disturbs the flame's teardrop shape.

To avoid smoking, the candle wick should be trimmed to 0.25 inches (0.6cm) each time it is used. Candles also should be burned away from drafts, air-conditioning vents, and open windows. If a candle keeps smoking, it is not burning properly. It should be extinguished, cooled, trimmed, and tested again later.

Now that you understand the elements of a candle and how it works, you are ready to try making your own candle!

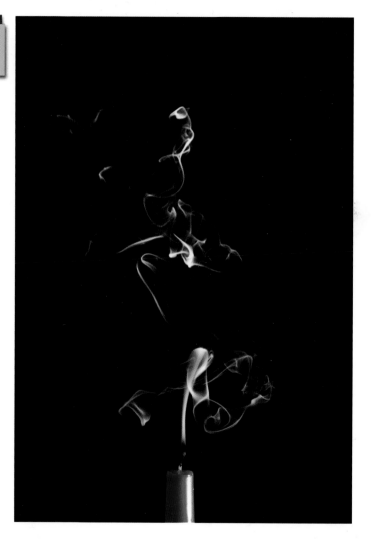

Chapter 3

Making Your Own Rolled Beeswax Candle

In this chapter you will learn the process for making a rolled beeswax candle. This is one of the simplest candles to make. You can make and decorate a rolled candle in less than an hour. All you need are a few candle-making supplies.

These are the materials you will need to make a rolled beeswax candle:

 Several honeycomb beeswax sheets You should be able to find these at your local craft or candle-making store. If not, an adult can help you order beeswax sheets from several online candle-making Web sites. A package of ten sheets that measure 16 inches by 8 inches (40.6cm by 20.3cm) costs between $13.00 and $15.00.

Square braided cotton wick The size of your wick depends on the size of the candle you plan to make. If the candle will be less than 2 inches (5.1cm) in diameter, choose a small wick. For 2 to 3 inches (5.1 to 7.6cm) in diameter, use a medium wick. Candles between 3 to 4 inches (7.6 to 10.2cm) in diameter work best with a large wick, and candles over 4 inches (10.2cm) in diameter should use an extra-large wick. You can find candlewicks at craft or candle-making stores or online. Four feet (1.2m) of wick costs about $2.00.

Hair dryer

Ruler

Scissors

Newspaper

Cookie cutters These can be used to cut shapes into the beeswax.

Steps to Make a Rolled Beeswax Candle

Step #1: Warm the wax

Before you begin, cover your work area, such as a kitchen table, with newspaper. Lay your first sheet of wax on the newspaper. Blow warm air from a hair dryer over the wax sheet for a minute or two. The warm air will soften the wax and make it more **pliable**. Do not heat your wax too long. You do not want it to melt!

Step #2: Cut the wax

Using scissors, cut your wax sheet the long way so that the sheet is the height you want your candle to be. You might want to use a ruler or another straight edge to help you cut in a straight, even line. Save the scrap wax; you can use it later for decorating your candle.

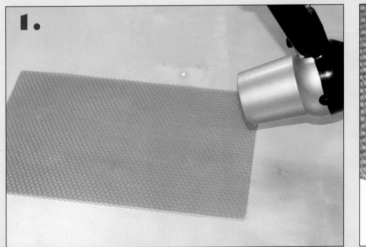

1.

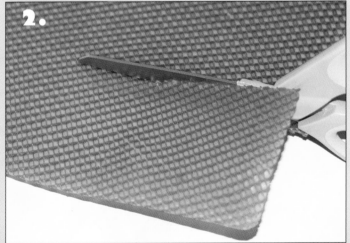

2.

Step #3: Place the wick

Place the shiny side of your wax sheet face down. Measure and cut a piece of wick so that about half an inch (1.3cm) of wick extends past the wax from the top and bottom. Lay the wick across one edge of the wax sheet. Carefully fold the wax over the wick. Try to keep the edges as round as possible. Slowly roll the wax sheet around the wick as you would roll a sleeping bag.

3.

Step #4: Roll it up

Continue to roll your candle slowly and carefully. Watch the edges of the candle to make sure you are rolling straight. Roll firmly so that your candle is tightly rolled. To make your candle's diameter larger, add a second and/or third sheet of beeswax. When adding a new sheet, press the sheet end against the ends of the previous sheet. Do not overlap the sheets; instead, place them against each other. If needed, heat the new sheet with the hair dryer to make it easier to roll. Continue rolling until your candle reaches the size you want.

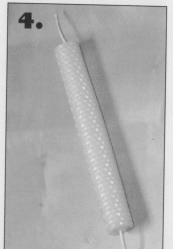

4.

Step #5: Finish the candle body

When you have finished rolling, you will need to seal the last sheet's edge to the candle so that it does not unroll. You can use your body heat to warm up the wax enough to seal it. Press your fingers gently along the wax sheet's edge. Press firmly along the entire edge until the wax is molded to the candle body. Do not press too hard though or you may damage your candle.

Stand your candle upright. If the base is slightly uneven, press firmly against a flat surface to even it. You may need to heat it slightly with the hair dryer to make the wax more pliable. Then use scissors to trim the candle wick. On the bottom of the candle, trim the wick so that it is even with the candle base. On the candle top, trim the wick to about 0.25 inches (0.6cm) long.

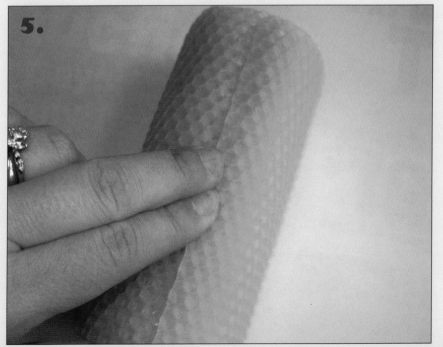
5.

Step #6: Decorate the candle

You can use wax sheets of different colors to decorate your candle. Use cookie cutters or scissors to cut out different shapes, stripes, and designs. Heat your decorations slightly with a hair dryer, then press them firmly into place on the body of your candle. When you have finished decorating, your candle is ready to light!

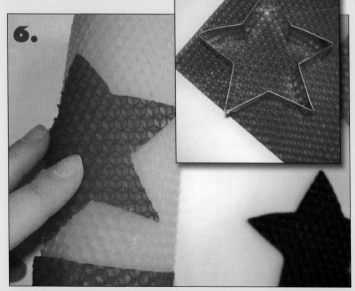

6.

Candle Safety Tips
A candle can be a fire hazard if burned incorrectly. Make sure you always follow these safety tips when burning a candle.

1. Never leave a burning candle unattended.
2. To protect tables and other surfaces, always burn your candle in a holder.
3. Burn your candle on a sturdy, heat resistant surface that is away from drafts and flammable materials. Remember to use a glass or ceramic holder and never set your candle directly on furniture.
4. Always keep burning candles out of the reach of young children and pets.
5. Stop burning the candle when only 0.5 inches (1.3cm) of wax is left.
6. Trim your wick to about 0.25 inches (0.6cm) to prevent smoking.
7. If your candle drips, check to see if there is a draft. Then move your candle to another safe location.

Lighting Your Candle

Before you light any candle, make sure you have your parents' permission and help. When burning your candle, knowing a few tips will help it burn properly. First, before you light the candle each time, trim the wick to about 0.25 inches (0.6cm) long. This will reduce the excess carbon that builds up on the wick and will prevent the candle's flame from burning too big.

Before you light your candle, you should also make sure you have enough time to burn it. The first time you light your candle, it should burn until the wax melts close to the outer edge of the candle. This will help your candle burn more evenly throughout its life. For candles that are 3 inches (7.6cm) or larger in diameter, this can take two or more hours.

While your candle burns, you can watch the wick and flame to see if you have a good burn. A candle that burns well will have a 1- to 2-inch- (2.5 to 5.1cm) long steady flame. A flickering or sputtering flame is a sign that your candle is not burning properly. Another sign of a good burn is how the wax melts. The hot wax should form a liquid pool around the wick. The liquid wax should not spill over the candle's edge. It also should be big enough for the wick to pull the liquid fuel up to the flame.

After burning, allow the candle to cool before storing. You should always store your candles in a cool, dark, and dry place. Taper candles should be stored flat so that they will not lose their shape. You should also avoid placing candles in direct sunlight or harsh in-door lighting. This might cause them to fade or soften. If your candle has dulled or faded, try gently rubbing it with a soft cloth. This can remove fingerprints and dust to restore its original sheen. With careful storing, your candle will be ready the next time you want to light it.

Mind Your Own Beeswax

Have you ever wondered where the phrase "mind your own beeswax" comes from? According to some researchers, the phrase arose centuries ago when wealthy women used beeswax as makeup. They spread the white paste over their faces to make them more beautiful. Yet on warm days, or if they stood too close to a fire, the wax makeup would start to melt. If another woman was caught staring, she would be told to "mind her own beeswax!" Around the same time, if a woman wearing beeswax makeup smiled, people said she "cracked a smile."

Chapter 4

Making Your Own Milk Carton Candle

In this chapter you will learn the process for making a milk carton candle. All you need are a few candle-making supplies, some milk cartons, and a stove. When making this type of candle, you will have to heat and melt a block of wax on the stove. You should ask an adult to help you with the hot wax.

These are the materials you will need to make a milk carton candle:

✓ **A block of candle wax.** You can find candle wax at your local craft or candle-making store. A 1.5-pound (0.68kg) block of wax costs about $8.00.

✓ **Candle wick.** For this project you may want to choose a cored wick. This type of wick has a core made of paper or wire that helps it stand straight while the melted wax hardens around it. The size of your wick depends on the size of the candle you plan to make. If the candle will be less than 2 inches (5.1cm) in diameter, choose a small wick. For 2 to 3 inches (5.1 to 7.6cm) in diameter, use a medium wick. Candles between 3 and 4 inches (7.6 to 10.2cm) in diameter work best with a large wick, and candles over 4 inches (10.2cm) in diameter should use an extra-large wick. You can find candle wicks at craft or candle-making stores as well as online. Four feet (1.2m) of wick costs about $2.00.

✓ **Candle dye.** You can find a range of colors at your local craft or candle-making store. One package of dye costs between $2.00 and $3.00 and will last for many candles.

✓ **Candle fragrance (optional).** If you want to add fragrance to your candle, you can find fragrance packets in your local craft store. One package costs between $2.00 and $3.00.

✓ **Two old pots or an old double boiler.** Melting candle wax can be messy, so ask your parents for two old pots to use. One pot should be slightly smaller than the other. Or, you can use an old double boiler.

✓ **Empty milk cartons.** Rinse the cartons and let them dry before use. You may also use juice or egg substitute cartons.

✓ **Pencils**

✓ **Scissors**

✓ **Wooden stirring stick**

✓ **Pot holders**

✓ **Knife**

✓ **Cutting board**

✓ **Newspaper**

Steps to Make a Milk Carton Candle

Step #1: Prepare the carton

Before you begin, cover your work area with newspaper. Using scissors, cut your milk carton to the desired height. The carton should be at least 1 inch (2.5cm) taller than you plan to make your candle. Make sure that your carton is dry and clean.

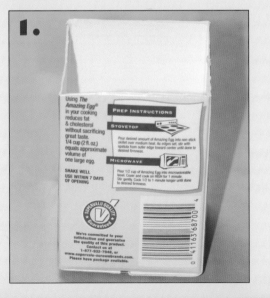

1.

Step #2: Melt the wax

Before you turn on the stove, ask an adult for help. Add water to the larger pot and place it on the stove. Place your block of wax in the smaller pot. Then place the smaller pot inside the larger pot. Or, you can use a double boiler to melt the wax. Turn on the stove to low heat. The wax will gradually melt to liquid form. Never leave the wax on the stove unattended.

2.

Hot Wax Safety Tips

To prevent injury, make sure you follow these safety tips when working with hot wax:

1. Always have the supervision of an adult.
2. Always heat the wax in a double boiler or use the two-pot method described on the previous page. Never let the water boil or overheat the wax.
3. Keep wax away from an open flame. It can start a fire.
4. If you splatter yourself with hot wax, submerge your skin in cold water until the wax is cool enough to remove by peeling it off.
5. Be very careful when pouring hot wax. Use a pot holder when handling hot pots and containers.
6. Never pour hot wax down the drain. Instead, pour it into cups or tins. When it hardens, remove from the tin or cup then store it in a plastic bag and reuse for your next candle project.
7. If a fire starts when you are making candles, turn off the heat source. To extinguish the fire, cover it with a pan lid, dump baking soda over it, or use a chemical fire extinguisher. Never use water to extinguish a wax fire. It may cause the wax to splatter and burn you.

Storing leftover wax in plastic bags will keep it ready for your next project.

Step #3: Add color and/or fragrance

If you want to add color and/or fragrance to your candle, use a knife and cutting board to shave small pieces from the block of candle dye or fragrance. Add these shavings to the melted wax. Stir all with a wooden stirring stick. To test your color, place a drop of the melted wax on a piece of white paper. Add more dye shavings until you reach the color you want.

Step #4: Pouring wax and placing a wick

Carefully pour the hot wax into the carton. Measure and cut a piece of wick that is about 1 inch (2.5cm) longer than the top of your container. Lower one end of the wick into the hot wax until it reaches the bottom of the container. Wrap the top of the wick around a wooden pencil or rod. Lay the pencil across the top of the carton, hanging the wick into the melted wax. Make sure to center the wick in the candle. Let the wax harden completely. It may take several hours.

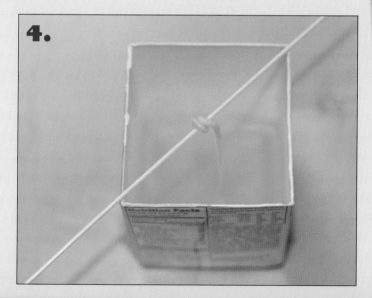

4.

Girl Scout Candle Ceremony

Candles are an important part of ceremonies for the Girl Scouts. Juliette Low, founder of the Girl Scouts, held one of the first candle-lighting ceremonies. Her troop was splitting up; some of the girls were moving away or spending more time helping their own families. Low wanted each girl to carry a special spark from the troop with her as she moved into the world. Low lit her candle and passed her flame to each girl. She asked them to keep the candles special and use them for other ceremonies to pass the flame to others. Today, many troop leaders hold a similar candle ceremony for their girls.

Step #5: Peel away the carton

Once the candle wax is completely hardened, peel the milk carton away from the candle. If it does not separate easily, you can slide a knife between the candle and carton to loosen it. Before you burn the candle, remember to trim the wick to be about 0.25 inches (0.6cm) long.

5.

Variation: A Layered Candle

You can also create a milk carton candle with different layers of color. Pour the first layer of wax into the carton. Place the candle wick according to step 4 on the previous page. Let the first layer of wax harden. Then add a second layer of wax in a different color. Repeat for more layers if desired.

Variation

Candle Superstitions

For years candle burning has been linked to magical rituals. As a result, many superstitions—in other words, beliefs not based on reason or facts—exist about candles. Which ones have you heard?

- Lighting a candle with your right hand brings good fortune. If the candle should go out immediately, however, bad luck will follow you.
- Never light a candle from a burning fire if you wish to be rich.
- Light a white candle (the color of protection) during a storm for safety.
- Lighting a candle at a birth, for a death, and on a birthday brings protection from evil.
- When a candle goes out during a ritual, a restless ghost is present.
- If a candle will not light, a storm is coming.
- If you see a ring in the candle flame, a marriage or engagement is coming soon.
- If there is a lump of soot in the wick of your candle, a stranger will soon visit.

Superstitions surround candles, including the importance of using your right hand to light one.

Candles produce a warm and welcoming light.

Light and Beauty

For centuries people have valued candles for their light and beauty. Candle making has also become an art, with candles being made in all shapes, sizes, and colors. With a little practice you can create these useful and decorative candles for your home, friends, and family.

Glossary

Advent (AD-vent): The period leading up to Christmas in the Christian Church's year.

brittle (BRIT-uhl): Likely to break, snap, or crack when under pressure.

congealed (kuhn-JEELD): Changed from fluid into solid form by cooling or freezing.

diameter (dahy-AM-i-ter): The length of a straight line from one edge of the circle to another edge passing through the center.

flax (flaks): A slender plant with narrow leaves and blue flowers that is grown for its fiber and seeds.

hydrocarbon (hahy-druh-KAHR-buhn): A substance made of the elements hydrogen and carbon.

indispensable (in-di-SPEN-suh-buhl): Something that is absolutely necessary.

piston (PIS-tuhn): A disk or cylinder that moves back and forth in a larger cylinder, as in pumps and compressors.

pitch (PICH): A dark, sticky substance that is made from tar or petroleum.

pliable (PLAHY-uh-buhl): Easily bent and flexible.

rancid (RAN-sid): Spoiled or rotted such as food.

retardant (ri-TAHR-dnt): Slowing down the speed of a chemical reaction.

secreted (see-CREE-ted): Made a substance from cells or bodily fluids.

shrine (SHRAHYN): A holy place that often contains sacred objects.

soot (SOOT): Black powder that is produced when a fuel such as coal, wood, or oil is burned.

stearic acid (STEER-ik AS-id): A common fatty acid found in tallow and other animal fats.

symbolic (sim-BAHL-ik): Standing for or representing something else.

synthetic (sin-THET-ik): Something that is made by humans rather than found in nature.

tallow (TAL-oh): Fat from cattle and sheep that is used mainly to make candles and soap.

wick (WIK): A twisted cord running through a candle that soaks up the fuel and burns when lit.

For More Information

Books

Abadie, Marie-Jeanne. *The Everything Candlemaking Book: Create Homemade Candles in House-Warming Colors, Interesting Shapes, and Appealing Scents.* Avon, MA: Adams Media, 2002.

Espino, Michelle. *Candlemaking for Fun and Profit.* NY: Crown Publishing Group, 2000.

Oppenheimer, Betty. *The Candlemaker's Companion: A Complete Guide to Rolling, Pouring, Dipping, and Decorating Your Own Candles.* North Adams, MA: Storey, 2004.

Web Sites

AHC arts & crafts (www.artistshelpingchildren.org). Look in this Web site's craft directory for a candle section that has instructions for several detailed candle-making projects for kids.

Candle and Soap Making Techniques (www.candletech.com). This Web site has several articles, including candle-making safety tips, instructions for making different types of candles, and how to choose candle fragrances and colors.

My Craft Book: Candle Making Instructions and Techniques

(www.mycraftbook.com/Candle_Making.asp). This Web site features several articles about candle making, candle safety and a variety of candle craft projects.

National Candle Association

(www.candles.org). The National Candle Association is the major trade association for the candle industry. It promotes the safe use and enjoyment of candles. Its Web site has information on the history of candles, how candles work, different types of candles, and safety tips.

Index

About the Author

Carla Mooney is the author of several books for young adults and children. She lives in Pittsburgh, Pennsylvania, with her husband and three children.